# INTRODUCTION

The guinea pig, which is also known as the cavy, ranks only a little way behind the rabbit as a popular pet. Its original homelands were the savannahs of northern South America. Exactly when it was introduced to Europe and the USA is not known for sure, but we can draw conclusions from history. During the 16th century the Spanish, Portuguese, and Dutch

## WHAT IS A GUINEA PIG?

The guinea pig, which has the scientific name of *Cavia porcellus*, is a small, almost tailless, rodent. Its closest relatives, other than wild guinea pigs, are porcupines, agoutis, chinchillas, and animals such as the coypu. There are about fourteen species of wild guinea pigs, and they are all native to

Guinea pigs are attractive and hardy little creatures that can make wonderful pets.

all had colonies in South America. Apart from gold and other precious minerals, the early explorers returned to Europe with any items they felt would be interesting and valuable. Exotic parrots started to appear in the homes of the wealthy, and it is probable that along with them went the guinea pig and other animals not known in Europe.

South America. Which one is the ancestor of the domesticated form is not known, because the domestication process was never recorded. However, it is generally thought that this honor goes to *C. aperea*, *C. fulgida*, or *C. tschudii*.

The order Rodentia is divided into a number of suborders, the guinea pig being in that called Hystricomorpha. The rabbit

If gradually introduced, guinea pigs will get along with most domestic pets.

(along with hares) is in the suborder known as Lagomorpha, while other pet rodents, such as rats, mice, and gerbils, are in the suborder Myomorpha. Collectively, the rodents comprise the largest number of species in the class Mammalia.

The main feature of a rodent is the possession of teeth designed to gnaw. This is possible because of the elongated incisor teeth, of which the guinea pig has two pairs. The lower jaw is very maneuverable, being able to move forward when gnawing, and backwards when grinding. Rodents have no canine teeth, instead there is a gap (called a diastema) between the incisors and the premolars. This allows the rodent to push its cheek skin into the gap and separate the front part of the mouth from the rear. It can then gnaw and select what food items it wishes to allow into the rear of the mouth, thus the digestive system.

Another feature of guinea pigs is that unlike most other rodents and mammals, their young are born fully furred and able to move around within hours after their birth. This survival strategy means that guinea pigs need only have small litters when compared with rabbits or mice. Their young are not as vulnerable as those of species whose babies are born blind, naked, and helpless. This is actually one of the guinea pig's merits, because it means you will not be overrun with unwanted offspring–as can often be the case with many other rodent species.

## WHY CALL THEM GUINEA PIGS?

The origin of the name guinea pigs has been lost in antiquity. It may be linked with the fact that guinea pigs are found, among other places, in the South American country of Guyana, which was a Dutch colony in the 16th century. Then again it could be that a port of call for returning ships from South America may have been Guinea, the former French colony situated in West Africa. More likely is the fact that "gulden" in German and Dutch meant golden, and some of the wild guinea pigs are of this color. Finally, the guinea was a golden coin used in England, and throughout its colonies. Maybe the guinea pig exchanged hands originally for twenty-one shillings (a guinea). The pig part of the name is easy to see because guinea pigs have a similar rounded rear end. They also run and squeal much after the fashion of little piglets. The term cavy is derived directly from the scientific name of *Cavia*, this being the genus for wild guinea pig species. The name guinea pig has of course found its way into popular language use as a term for anything that is being used for experiments. Sadly, these delightful little rodents have, along with mice, rats, and rabbits, a long history of being used as laboratory subjects.

Guinea pigs are scientifically known as *Cavia porcellus* and that is where their common name (cavies) originates.

## GENERAL PET ATTRIBUTES

Guinea pigs have many attributes as pets, and virtually no faults. They are small in size and can be fed a wide range of foods that will cost you little or nothing. They are quiet, yet have a sufficient range of vocal tones to let you know how they are feeling. They are extremely clean in their personal habits and are never aggressive with people or other animals. If they have any drawback at all it is perhaps that they are very retiring little creatures. This means they are easily frightened by noises or sudden movements, so will scamper for cover at the slightest hint of what they perceive to be danger.

When fully grown, a guinea pig will weigh between one and three pounds and will be about eight to ten inches long.

They are very popular exhibition animals, there being about forty varieties from which you can choose. These include not only different colors and coat patterns, but also differing fur types, some being smoothcoated, some covered with rosettes, and others sporting longer coats. Guinea pigs can be small or large, but the differences in size are relatively minor when compared to rabbits or dogs. You will therefore not find a guinea pig which grows to a size that you had not anticipated.

Guinea pigs get along extremely well with other pets, especially rabbits, but they can be vulnerable to dogs, foxes, coyotes and even cats, so you must be sure they are safe from these if they are kept in an outdoor situation. While females, called sows, can be mixed in numbers, the same is not true of males, called boars. Boars will get along fine while they are immature, but as adults are prone to fight each other. Such fights can be very serious if the boars sense there are females in the vicinity. A boar can be run quite happily with any number of sows.

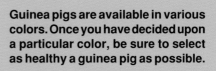

Guinea pigs are available in various colors. Once you have decided upon a particular color, be sure to select as healthy a guinea pig as possible.

If your guinea pig is outdoors, it is susceptible to a number of dangers. Take the necessary precautions before you let it loose.

# ACCOMMODATIONS

Guinea pigs are not difficult to cater for in their housing needs providing you make due consideration for what those needs are. Unfortunately, a large number of owners condemn their pets to a very unhappy life because they fail to ensure their hamsters, gerbils, mice, and guinea pigs, are kept in housing that is far too small to be regarded as adequate. This situation is of historical origin, and also reflects the fact that these pets are inexpensive, so many owners do not want to

While broad daylight is beneficial, do not expose your guinea pig to intense heat which could lead to illness.

pets have the sort of accommodations needed. The essentials for a guinea pig are that it is protected from both damp areas and drafts. Beyond this their accommodations should reflect the amount of time that you are able to devote to them. If your time is limited, you should provide the sort of housing that allows them ample room to exercise in.

It is a fact of life that most pet animals, such as rabbits, invest much cash into housing. With a little thought and imagination, you can provide excellent housing for your pet–it does not need to cost a fortune.

## INSIDE OR OUT?

Guinea pigs have adapted well to the temperate climates of Britain, the USA, Canada, Australia, and other countries. However, the winter months of these countries can be quite severe. If guinea pigs are to be kept outdoors their housing must be robust. If they are kept indoors, for example in a garden shed or similar outbuilding, the hutches can be less substantial, because they will not have to endure rain, snow, strong sunlight, or cold winds. Most breeders keep their guinea pigs indoors, but this author maintained outdoor enclosures for a number of years, and these proved very successful. However, outdoor housing is not without its problems. For one thing, chores are no fun in the winter months. The number of guinea pigs that can be kept is probably more restricted because of the space needed for runs.

The cost of the housing is substantially more expensive because of the extra thickness of timber needed and the cost of link fencing small enough to prevent the pets escaping. On balance, the first time guinea pig owner is advised to house their pets in an indoor situation, with maybe an outdoor area being fenced off for them to exercise in during the warmer months, and when they are under supervision (so cats, foxes and their like do not jump into the enclosure in order to have a meal on plump little piggies). This situation can be overcome by having the outdoor area covered with weld wire, rather like an aviary, but of a much lower height.

**THE HUTCH**

The hutch described here is

**Be sure to put your guinea pig in a safe, secure spot from other neighborhood pets when outdoors.**

**Guinea pigs do enjoy the outdoors. Make sure there is careful supervision so your pet does not run away and become lost.**

actually one that would be suitable for outdoor use. Clearly, if it was to be an indoor unit, certain features of it could be redesigned (for example the roof) in order to make savings. In its most simple form a hutch is a box structure with a weld wire front. For a single guinea pig, the size should be a minimum of 62 cm long x 38 cm wide x 31 cm high (24 x 15 x 12 in). Such dimensions, especially this length, really provide only minimal living accommodations that would be used indoors. You could greatly improve on this by adding another 31 cm (12 in) to the length and inserting a wooden, or Plexiglass, partition in order to create a separate sleeping area for your pets. Better still would be to add another 23 cm (9 in) section that would become the latrine area. This can be added onto the opposite end of the accommodations, thus leaving the larger central area for feeding and playing in.

A solid wooden external door can be added to the sleeping quarters so this is easily cleaned out. Small arch openings connect the bedroom to the living area, and likewise to the latrine, and from there to the outside. This opening can be a door, so that the guinea pigs can be retained in the hutch if desired. The hutch should be placed on substantial legs so that it is at least 15 cm (6 in) off the floor. This allows air to circulate beneath the floor, and eliminates the risk of rodents taking up residence under the hutch.

From the latrine, or the exercise area, a ramp can be added that allows the guinea pigs access to their enclosure–be this in your garden or in a shed. The ramp should have wooden cross members on it so the pets do not slide. The hutch roof should be of the pitched or sloping design in order to carry rain away. It is best if it overhangs the side walls, thus giving them some protection from the elements. In an outdoor situation the roof should be covered with roofing felt, or similar cladding, so it is really waterproof.

**Guinea pigs must have water available at all times. The most convenient way of accomplishing this is to supply your pet with a water bottle such as the one this hamster is using. Photo courtesy of Penn Plax.**

## EXERCISE ENCLOSURES

All guinea pig and rabbit owners should have one or more adequate exercise areas for their stock. This keeps them in a fit and healthy condition. As important, it is essential for their psychological well being. They do not like being imprisoned in a hutch for long periods any more than you or I would enjoy being restricted to a single room for days on end. This results in stress, and stress greatly increases the chances of ill health and breeding problems.

If your pets are kept in a shed it is easy to provide an area for the guinea pigs to play in. You should also have an outdoor area for them to graze or play on during the warmer months. This can be in the form of a permanent enclosure covered with wire weld, or in a movable unit that is made of a framework covered with weld wire. This can be box shaped or an A-frame structure, and it should have a wire weld floor. This allows the guinea pigs to graze without any risk of them escaping. If they are left unattended for any length of time be sure there is a shaded area to their enclosure, as guinea pigs can suffer from sunburn just as you can.

## PLAYTHINGS

In a permanent indoor or outdoor enclosure there is ample scope for you to provide an interesting area for your pets to play in. Even in a roomy cage you could provide a single plaything. In an enclosure you can lay

One of the greatest characteristics of guinea pigs is their friendliness. They will warm up to just about anyone.

ceramic sewage pipes on the ground. The guinea pigs will enjoy scampering in and out of these. They also enjoy running up and down rocks and over small logs. A small soil area will be enjoyed by guinea pigs who will often cool themselves by laying on this. If you decide to build a tunnel network for the guinea pigs to run in and out of, be sure that this is always above ground level. This overcomes the possible risk of it flooding while they are in it, should there be a sudden downpour of rain.

Many guinea pig owners never experience the full pleasure of their pets because the pets do not have the facilities that enable them to be seen at their best. Given roomy enclosures of interesting design guinea pigs will run around playing and squeaking. They love exploring–as long as they are familiar with a good escape route back to the safety of their hutch, or a suitable place of refuge. Our rabbits and guinea pigs, who shared similar accommodations, found snow to be a wonderful thing to play in for a short while, then they would scamper back to the warmth of their cozy hutch.

**FLOOR COVERINGS**

The most popular floor coverings for a hutch and indoor enclosure are sawdust and wood shavings. You could also use layers of paper, or the granulated paper now available for pet bedding. Sand is a poor cover because it can stain the coats of the guinea pigs, and is also an

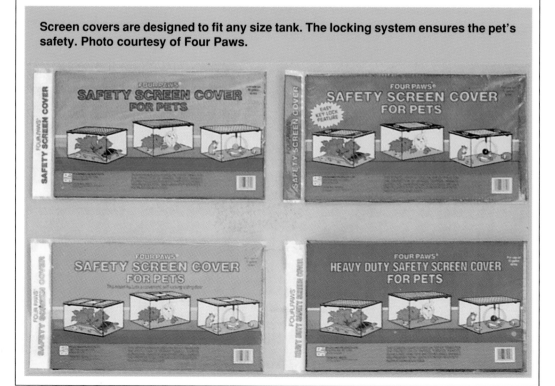

Screen covers are designed to fit any size tank. The locking system ensures the pet's safety. Photo courtesy of Four Paws.

It is in the best interest of both you and the guinea pig to purchase all of its accessories before your pet's arrival. This will make a much easier transition for the guinea pig into your home.

irritant. Straw has little absorbency and can damage the eyes of guinea pigs via its sharp ends. The dust from sawdust can cause irritation to the eyes and nose of guinea pigs, and it also tends to cling to the soft foods, such as mashes or fruits and vegetables. The ideal covering is thus not available, but sawdust covered with wood shavings, or granulated paper and wood shavings, are possibly the best options.

For the bedding area the ideal is hay on a paper base. Use brown paper as this will not soil the coats of light colored guinea pigs with ink from newsprint. Paper provides a warm base while quality hay–which must never smell musty, nor show signs of mold on it—will provide not only very soft bedding, but is also an important food item. Especially during the winter, be sure the guinea pigs have plenty of hay. It should be checked daily. They will make a nice nest of this. It is not as important during the warmer months, but should still be sufficient for them to make a good lining on top of the paper.

### ROUTINE CLEANING

The hutch should be cleaned as often as its condition suggests, based on the number of occupants, and most certainly once each week. A paint scraper, a stiff handbrush, a dustpan, and a yard brush are the items you will need. The paint scraper will enable you to get into the corners of the hutch to scrape out damp sawdust. Then it can be given a brisk brush with the handbrush, with all the debris being swept into a plastic sack or a large cardboard box. Guinea pig droppings make a fine compost– but do not have a compost heap

Wood chips can be used to line the tray of the cage. They will help to absorb urine and thereby contribute to the cleanliness of the dwelling unit and consequently to the good health of the animal(s). Photo courtesy of Kaytee.

Your guinea pig should be healthy, bright-eyed, active, and alert.

anywhere near the hutch as it will attract flies, and is a prime source of bacterial colonization.

The latrine area is better for being cleaned every two or three days. A few layers of paper under the sawdust will help protect the wooden floor from becoming soaked–which would otherwise quickly rot. Periodically, during warm weather, it is wise to give the entire hutch interior a wash down using hot water containing an acaracide to the paint. This will greatly reduce the risk of mites and other parasites establishing colonies in the crevices of the woodwork. The exterior timber of an outdoor hutch must be routinely repainted, or otherwise preserved, to ensure it retains its water repellent properties.

By using a little imagination you can easily provide your guinea pigs with an interesting

**Straw is not an appropriate material for bedding. Not only does straw have little absorbency, but its sharp ends can injure your pet.**

a disinfectant. Ensure it is really dry before introducing the guinea pigs back to it. If you plan to be a breeder it is prudent to have at least two or three spare cages so that there are always such cages laying fallow for a number of weeks. It would also be sound husbandry to repaint the interior of the cages each year, and to add home that is both very functional from their viewpoint, but also practical to keep clean from yours. You are not bounded by any conventions that dictate a hutch must be a given shape, so if you are a handy person it is possible to create a home that looks good, yet offers interest to its residents.

# STOCK SELECTION

There are a number of questions you need to answer before going out and purchasing stock. These should be the subject of careful consideration so that you increase your chance of obtaining the guinea pig best suited to your needs. We will discuss the following in the order cited: Age to purchase, which sex, choosing healthy stock, which variety, and selecting quality stock.

### AGE TO PURCHASE

The age at which you purchase your guinea pig(s) will reflect the reasons you want the guinea pig in the first place. It will also be influenced by the situation in your home. Guinea pigs become independent of their mother when they are about four weeks old, so they are able to go to new homes any time after this. However, if you intend to become a breeder, or to exhibit your pets, you may find it better to purchase mature examples whose quality is established, rather than hoped for.

Proven breeders or show winners will of course cost more than juveniles of unproven status, but even quite good guinea pigs should not break

There is something for everyone when you take into consideration all of the different types of guinea pigs.

your bank account. If the guinea pigs are simply to be house pets in a home that has very young children you may be better to start off with a youngster of at least eight or more weeks of age. Such an individual will be much more established than one that has barely been weaned from its mother. Indeed, an adult that is mature and used to being

due course. If this situation is not wanted you should obtain two females. I strongly suggest that two guinea pigs are purchased because these are very social animals and will provide company for each other. The upkeep of two is really little more than with one, and two will give you much more pleasure.

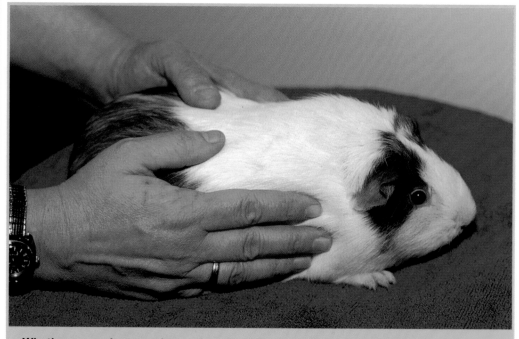

**Whether you select a male or a female, either sex will make a good pet.**

handled may be the very best choice. Pet shops and breeders invariably have a good stock of such examples.

### WHICH SEX?

Either sex will make a fine pet so this aspect is not really important. If you have one of each sex there is clearly every possibility that you will be presented with youngsters in

If you plan to become a breeder then you will want at least a trio of guineas–one boar and two females. You can keep a male with any number of females, but housing two boars together is not recommended. They will fight constantly in the presence of females, and even if none of the opposite sex are present one will tend to bully the other.

## CHOOSING HEALTHY STOCK

Whether you plan to have pet guinea pigs or quality show and breeding stock, they must, first and foremost, be healthy. Before even inspecting the stock you should assess the general conditions under which they are living. Cramped, damp, or overcrowded living quarters in which there are clear signs that cleaning is not a high priority should see you leaving and seeking out a better supplier. The only way to remove uncaring breeders and suppliers from the hobby is to never support them.

Assuming you are satisfied with the supplier you should next take a general view of the stock on offer. A good breeder or pet shop will not have any unhealthy stock mixed with healthy individuals so, if an unwell example is noticed, you are advised not to purchase from that place. This is because the rest of the stock has obviously been exposed to the unwell specimen. It may thus have contracted the problem, even if it does not display signs of it at that time.

Watch the guinea pigs for a few minutes to see they are all moving about without any indication of difficulty such as lameness. You want lively individuals, not those that seem very nervous–given that all guinea pigs are very cautious when approached and will quickly scamper away from you if they can. Having fixed on one or two that appeal, the next thing is to examine them.

The eyes and nose should show no signs of a discharge. The eyes should be round and bright. The teeth should be neatly aligned so the uppers just touch the lowers. If they are out of alignment this is called malocclusion and will result in the teeth continuing to grow such that they may even grow into the jaws. Such situations will obviously affect the animal's ability to eat properly. Should it occur, it can be corrected by your vet periodically trimming the teeth, but it is obviously better to have guinea pigs that have good dental work in the first place. Misalignment of the incisors is an inherited feature, so this is taboo in stock required for breeding.

The anal region of the guinea pig should be clean and in no way stained or covered with dried fecal matter, which would clearly suggest a present or recent problem. The fur should be carefully inspected for any signs of lice or fleas. Brush it against its lie and watch for any parasites that dart away into the fur. Small blackish specks near the rump and the ears are flea dirt, and indicate their presence. Lice are grayish creatures that move more slowly through the fur. Be very thorough when inspecting mature Peruvians or Shelties, as their long coat is a prime site for parasites.

A particular thing to look for in guinea pigs are small areas devoid of fur. These are usually the result of fungal infection and this is very difficult to eradicate.

Any bald areas should give you reason to overlook that individual and any other guinea pigs it is living with. The fur should be sleek and glossy in all varieties other than the rough coated Abyssinian. The body of a guinea pig should be nicely filled with flesh, though very young stock will not be as well filled out as will the mature specimen.

## WHICH VARIETY?

If the guinea pig is to be a pet it does not need to be any of the recognized varieties. Cross breeds are just as good as the varieties, and can often be very pleasing in their colors. This said, you may want a particular color or coat type in which case a purebred will be needed. Do bear in mind that

Every guinea pig is unique! Your tastes and preferences should be compatible with that of your pet.

No guinea pig should look skinny, nor should the head appear "snippy." The ears will display a crinkled look, the extent of this varying according to both the age and the quality of the individual. The rump should be nicely rounded, while the legs and feet should show no signs of sores which would suggest poor living conditions.

the longcoated Peruvian and Sheltie require special attention. On this account they are not recommended as a pet animal because the coat invariably becomes matted and clogged with dirt and fecal matter, aspects not always appreciated when the guinea pig is purchased as a juvenile.

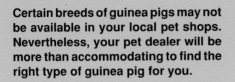

Certain breeds of guinea pigs may not be available in your local pet shops. Nevertheless, your pet dealer will be more than accommodating to find the right type of guinea pig for you.

**SELECTING QUALITY STOCK**

You cannot select quality guinea pigs by reading about them in a book, no matter how detailed the text is. Assessing a good example of any form of livestock can only come from the experience gained from having studied literally thousands of them over a period of time. Even then, it does not follow you will local to you. Keep in mind that simply obtaining good looking stock is only a small part of establishing a good stud. What is more important is how typical that stock is of that produced by the breeder. You want guinea pigs that come from a proven line, not "sparklers" that are the result of hit and miss breeding.

**Regardless of whether you purchase a shorthaired of longhaired guinea pig, there should be no bald spots.**

then, it does not follow you will have good judgment, which is why some exhibitors win consistently while others do not.

If you want to purchase quality guinea pigs the way to proceed is to attend a number of exhibitions. Talk with judges and exhibitors who specialize in the variety that appeals to you. Try to locate a breeder who is

Such guinea pigs may be quite useless from a breeding viewpoint, because they may not pass on their own good looks. A good breeder will have detailed records of their program, and their stock should be of a uniform standard, not showing great variation which would indicate random breeding.

It is thus a case of doing a lot of homework on breeders, then placing your faith in the one selected. You are advised to commence by purchasing all of your initial stock from one source. There is little merit in crossing differing lines until such crosses are needed, which the variety wanted. However, just how well they survive from the moment you take them from the breeder or pet shop is up to you. Very often, first-time owners will complain about a supplier when the problem was that they failed to provide the guinea pig with the correct food,

If you are keeping more than one guinea pig in your home, it is very wise to house each one separately.

will be some time after you are well established. A factor often compromised by many livestock breeders is the question of breeding vigor. This is the ability of the parents to produce strong litters with a good survival rate.

If you follow the advice given in this chapter you should end up with healthy guinea pigs of accommodations, and general care. If you do experience any initial difficulties in respect of the health of your newly acquired pet, do not delay in doing something about it. Contact the supplier first and if they do not satisfy your queries, call your veterinarian (and find another supplier for any further stock).

# NUTRITION

Guinea pigs, like most rodents, are herbivorous in their dietary needs. This means they eat vegetables, plants, fruits, grain, and its by-products. Like all living forms they also need water, which should be available to them at all times. Guinea pigs are unusual animals in that, along with humans, apes and monkeys, they are unable to synthesize vitamin C in their bodies. It is thus essential that this vital ingredient is always present in their diet. If they eat plenty of fruits and vegetables this need will be met. Before discussing the diet in more detail let us first consider other aspects of the feeding regimen.

## FOOD AND WATER CONTAINERS

It is not important what sort of dish you place the food in, but it will be found that heavy crock pots made for rabbits and cats are the most suitable. This is because lighter dishes, such as saucers or plastic dishes, are likely to be toppled over as the guinea pigs place their front feet on the edge of the dish. The result will be the food will be scattered among the sawdust or other floor covering. Use one pot for fresh foods, such as vegetables and fruits, and another one for the oats and bran.

Water can be supplied in a similar pot, or via one of the automatic dispensers available from all pet stores. These are inverted bottles which are clipped onto the hutch front. They contain a ball bearing that when

When your guinea pig is eating from a bowl, heavy feeding dishes are highly recommended.

Obviously, clean water is a must to ensure the life of your guinea pig and should be always available to your pet.

licked releases the water. Until you are sure your pets know how to use such dispensers it is best to provide water in a pot as well. During the winter the drop in temperature can freeze the ball bearing to the tube it is located in, so always check this is free. To be sure of the water supply, a daily pot in cold weather is advised for guinea pigs in outdoor situations.

If your guinea pigs have a spacious hutch it may be possible for you to include a feeding station in it. This is merely an area that is kept free of sawdust by a low retaining batten of wood. The food pots are placed in this, and there should be enough room for the guineas to take the food out of the pot and consume it nearby. In this way the food is not dropped into the floor covering as would normally happen. Another useful item in a spacious hutch would be a hay rack. This can be used for wild plants (which can be supplied whole, including the roots). You can purchase various sized models made from plastic.

**WHEN TO FEED**

It is not important when your guinea pigs are fed during the day as long as you stick to a set time. They, like us, are creatures of habit, and look forward to their food reasonably on time. They will show their anticipation of their meals by running around giving out high pitched squeaks on your approach. It is thus a case of fitting in their feeding schedule with your own work timetable. The best time to feed fresh foods and mashes is first thing in the morning, or in the late afternoon. This is especially so if the guinea pigs are housed outdoors. By supplying such foods at these times reduces the risk of it souring during the hot midday period. Oats, bran, and pellets can be supplied more or

not purchase large quantities of oats and bran such that there might be the risk of it going "off" through dampness or contamination by rodents. Store grain in a dry container, not in open bags or sacks. Fresh foods, such as greens or fruits, should not be overripe, nor left exposed to flies. Always wash such foods

As the weather gets warmer, guinea pigs will want to drink more water to keep themselves refreshed.

less on an ad lib basis, so it is simply a case of topping up their dish as it is emptied. Do wash all food containers each day, this applying to water vessels as well.

### FEED CLEAN & FRESH

A cardinal rule that should be adhered to when feeding guinea pigs is that the food should always be clean and fresh. Do

before feeding them to your pets. This is especially important with vegetation gathered either in your garden or from the countryside. These may have been subjected to insecticidal sprays, or may have been contaminated by fumes from vehicles.

Never leave fresh foods down for the guinea pigs to eat for

longer than one day. Any uneaten after this time should be discarded. Do remember that uneaten mashes cannot be stored after they have been served to your pets. They should be mixed fresh for each serving, and any excess placed in the refrigerator to be used the following day. That taken from the fridge should be fully thawed before being served.

**A TYPICAL MENU**

The grain part of the menu is usually crushed oats and bran, but flaked maize and any other grain crops can be fed to your pets. The by-products of these, such as breakfast cereals and bread, can

If you give your guinea pig greenfoods, make sure to wash beforehand to get rid of any insecticides.

also be included. Toasted or baked bread is beneficial for the guinea pigs as it provides a hard food which will help keep their teeth in good shape. Dog biscuits are useful for the same reason. Cookies and cakes are enjoyed by guinea pigs, but limit these sweet items and feed them as treats.

Vegetables suited to guinea pigs are all of those likely to be found in the kitchen. Carrots, cabbages, beans, peas, spinach, broccoli, parsnips, swedes, and even beets will be eaten according to individual taste and appetites. Potatoes should be boiled first and can then be given in pieces or in a mash. You can try your pets on any fruits that you would eat, apples being a standard favorite. Mix a small salad for the guinea pigs and watch which fruits they obviously like best– these will be the ones eaten first.

The potential list of favored wild plants is extensive and includes dandelion, shepherd's purse, coltsfoot, bramble, plantain, any wild grasses, clover, and chickweed. Poisonous plants to avoid are any that grow from bulbs, together with the obvious ones, such as deadly nightshade, buttercup, laburnum, and scarlet pimpernel. The golden rule to apply is "if in doubt leave it out." If you feed a wide selection of wild plants, any minor toxins eaten will usually be counteracted by another plant–which is why it is so important to

can purchase this in small bags, or you could locate a local farmer who sells it by the bale. Be sure it is good quality and smells fresh. It will include various wild plants in it. Reject any that show signs of mold or smells musty.

A final point of importance

**The more vitamins you provide in a guinea pig's diet, the less problems you will have on your hands concerning your guinea pig's health.**

always supply your pets with a good selection of foods from which to choose. This also ensures there will be no vitamins or minerals lacking in the diet. The petals of numerous garden flowers are enjoyed by guinea pigs. Among these are daisies, marigolds and sunflowers.

Hay is the basic plant food that you should ensure is always available to your guinea pigs. You

where wild plants are concerned, though it applies equally to most food items, is that they should never be fed suddenly in quantity. This can lead to scouring, a condition symptomized by diarrhea. When wild plants become available in the spring, feed them sparingly at first, but on a build up basis. Likewise, as the season ends, begin to reduce the amount of

There are a variety of foods that your guinea pig will enjoy.

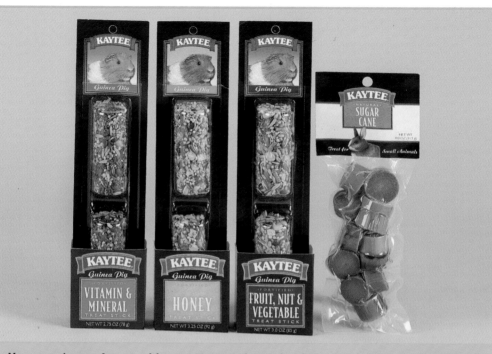

You can choose from a wide assortment of treat foods for your guinea pig, which will appreciate variety in its diet. Pet shops stock guinea pig treats as well as all kinds of other food items for guinea pigs. Photo courtesy of Kaytee.

plants likely to become unavailable during the winter months. In this way there is no sudden change in the diet, and you reduce the likelihood of stomach upsets.

## MASHES

You can concoct any number of recipes in order to prepare a mash for your pets. The basic ingredients will be crushed oats, and bran. To these you can add such items as chopped boiled eggs, grated cheese, mashed potatoes, nuts and seeds, and assorted chopped fruits and vegetables. Mix these all together in a bowl, then add just a little warm water. This should only be enough to bring the ingredients together so the mash is moist, not a sloppy mess! You could add a beef extract to the water if required. Milk can be used as the liquid and you can even add ingredients such as honey. Care is needed with either of these because milk sours very quickly, while honey attracts wasps. These can put your guinea pigs totally off eating the mash.

## DRY PELLETS & COMMERCIAL FOODS

Pelleted rabbit and guinea pig foods can be purchased from your local pet store. These are formulated to be complete diets, so feed them with care otherwise your plump guinea pigs may become obese. Although complete diets, I always feel they look boring and am always suspicious of any food that claims to be "complete." It has been established that some of these total diets are in fact lacking in some needed compounds, so they are best regarded as useful supplements. The big advantage of pellets is that they do not attract flies, so they can be left out for longer periods than other foods. Further, they are supplemented with essential vitamins. Store them carefully because once damp, they can be dangerous.

You can purchase packs of guinea pig foods, and these are usually fortified with vitamin C, which rabbit foods are not. They are convenient if you only have one or two pets. A breeder would find them an expensive way to feed his or her stock, so such people are best purchasing each item separately from their pet store or grain merchant.

**SUPPLEMENTS**

There are many protein, vitamin and mineral supplements available today–not all necessarily packaged for guinea pigs. If you feed your pets a wide ranging diet that already includes proteins (milk, cheese, eggs), vitamins (all greens and fruits) and carbohydrates (grain products), you should have no need to supply concentrated supplements. Indeed, an excess of any vitamin or mineral can actually be deleterious to your pet's health, because it upsets the absorption rate of other compounds.

If you feel that your guinea pig's coat seems lackluster, or shows some other symptom that may suggest nutritional deficiency, do discuss the matter with your vet before you purchase any of the many tonics and supplements. The problem may not be nutritional, so feeding

The main part of your guinea pig's diet should be dry feed that is formulated especially for guinea pigs. Photo courtesy of Kaytee.

supplements may actually make matters worse.

## WATER

Most people pay little attention to the quality of water supplied to their pets. This is because we all assume water is water, and it is quite safe providing it is from the faucet. However, the quality of water does differ significantly from one region, or country, to another. The various water authorities treat this with many chemicals to ensure it is safe for us to drink, added to which water does vary naturally in terms of its calcium content. What might not adversely affect our health may well do so to animals which are much smaller. In their case, excess quantities of certain chemicals can cause problems. In goldfish and koi for example, local water has been known to produce serious conditions in the fish, while in various cage birds, breeders are beginning to appreciate that the water given to stock can adversely affect the birds.

## FEEDING PHILOSOPHY

Feeding any form of livestock is not a science, though a basic understanding of the role of various foods is beneficial. It is more a matter of applying common sense and ensuring the food represents a balance of items that are fed in a fresh state. Never be afraid to experiment with items to see if your pets like them. A final point is that should your guinea pigs appear to be obese, do not withhold food from them. The remedy is to reduce the quantity. If food is withheld this may adversely affect the production of vitamins that your guinea pigs synthesize during digestion, and this could cause problems. Where feeding is concerned everything should be done gradually, so the guinea pig's digestive system is never subjected to sudden changes. It is sudden changes that usually causes problems.

The feeding of guinea pigs is relatively simple: Feed fresh and clean!

# PRACTICAL BREEDING

Breeding from your guinea pigs is a very interesting part of the hobby, but should be given some thought before being undertaken. You will need to consider if your pets are of good enough quality to be bred from, for there is little point in breeding for their own sake. Your objective should be to produce progressively better examples, rather than simply to perpetuate a species which is not in short supply. You should also consider the fact that you must have the extra accommodations to house the offspring, depending on how many individuals you plan to breed from. Finally, there is the matter of disposing of the surplus stock generated, though fortunately this is usually not a problem with these popular pets.

## SEXING

From their appearance, guinea pigs do not differ significantly with respect to the sexes. The boar is often larger, but this is not a reliable guide as it is a relative situation. There are large and

You can really gain a better understanding of guinea pigs from breeding pigs as pets or for exhibition.

small males and females. The only reliable way for you to sex these animals is to inspect their genital organs. This is done by carefully placing your hand on the guinea pig's back and then turning it over so its underparts are facing upwards. In a mature individual the testes of the male will be quite visible, but in the juvenile these will not have descended into the scrotal sacs. With a youngster you must therefore place your thumb and index finger either side of the genital orifice and press down and outwards very gently. This will extrude the penis of the male. In the female there is a small slit.

## BREEDING AGE

Guinea pigs are mature when about three months old, but it is wise to allow the sow an extra month or so, at least, before letting her breed. The boar is better when older because males mature more slowly, even if they are sexually adult at an earlier age. In fact, neither sex is physically fully mature until they are twelve or more months of age, and maximum weight is not reached until they are about 18 months of age. When breeding, it is sound policy to pair an established boar or sow to a young mate. The breeding life of guinea pigs will be in the order of three or four years for sows, and a little longer for boars. However, as individuals approach their later breeding life, the vigor and number of the offspring steadily falls.

In most forms of livestock breeding it has become quite normal to use younger and younger animals to breed from, and the merits of this are often stated. The drawbacks are not always given, because the full effect of the mother's physical state, related to age, is not known. Very few detailed studies have been made on this. The case in respect of polydactyly in guinea pigs is one of the rare instances where scientific study has been made, and it should give breeders reason to compile information based on their own breeding results.

## BREEDING CONDITION

This term relates to the physical condition of both the boar and the sow, especially the sow. If a sow is overweight and under exercised, it obviously increases the risk that problems during birth might occur. Preparing a sow for breeding is a continuum, not something you turn on a few weeks before the sow is due to have babies. From the outset of purchasing a potential breeding guinea pig, you must ensure it has lots of exercise. Its diet must be balanced, and it should not be in a situation where it is likely to get stressed–such as cramped quarters, or close proximity to anything that obviously frightens it (machines, other animals, or their like).

The diet can be adjusted about eight weeks before a birth is anticipated. You can feed the sow some bread soaked in milk, and can increase somewhat the protein element of the diet. Eggs, cheese, milk, and high protein

**Chances are that the sow will give birth to her young during the night. If you know she is expecting soon, be wary of this.**

powders are all items that will ensure the sow is not lacking in essential amino acids which are vital to the growing embryo. The sow can otherwise be allowed to live a normal life. There is no need to confine her, because exercise keeps her fit–she will adjust her physical activity according to how she feels. At some point before the sow is due to produce a litter, it is usual to remove her back to her own accommodations. This eliminates the slight risk that the boar might attack the newly born guinea pigs. It can be added that boars do make very tolerant fathers if they and the sow live in spacious quarters.

## BREEDING DATA

The estrus period (that time when the female is receptive to being mated) of the sow lasts for 14-17 days. The sow can be placed with the boar in his quarters and left with him until she shows obvious signs of a weight gain. You can calculate roughly when she would be due to produce her litter, then remove the boar a couple of weeks prior to this. The problem with this is that it could be two or three weeks after the sow has been introduced before the boar actually mates with her. There is also the problem that if the sow has only two or three babies she may show no signs of pregnancy until almost the time they are due to be born, the more so if she is a big sow.

Your calculations could thus be wide of the mark, but nonetheless it gives you a very approximate time period to work with. The gestation period in guinea pigs can range from 59-72 days, though 63 is the accepted time. Offspring born towards or at the extremes of the gestation period will often be stillborn, that is, dead at birth. The average litter size will be 3-4, but guinea pigs can have up to 10 babies, though this would be very rare. Many may only have 1-2, so do not worry if the litter is small.

The gestation period is long (over twice that of many rodents) because the offspring are born fully furred with their eyes open and able to run around within a hour or so after birth. They are able to nibble at foods almost from birth, and can actually start feeding on solid foods within 24 hours. The female nurses the babies for about 4-5 weeks. She has only two nipples, but copes quite well because of the fact that the youngsters can eat independently at such an early age, so are not totally preoccupied with obtaining milk all the while.

## THE BIRTH

The actual birth of the offspring usually happens during the night, so the first sign you will know of is seeing a number of babies scampering around. At this time you should examine them and check whether there are any dead babies in the nest made by the mother. If a youngster appears to be dead, do double check that this is so. Sometimes a brisk rubbing in your hands can recover a youngster on the brink of dying (maybe through it having become chilled).

A sow may eat a baby that has been born deformed in some way. This is a quite natural happening and is nature's way of ensuring the survival of the fittest. It also removes the possibility of a youngster dying, and thus decaying, in the nest area. It is not unknown for sows to eat their offspring. This can happen for a variety of reasons. The sow may be very young and panics at the sight of her own offspring. She may be undernourished and has an inborn mechanism that tells her she will be unable to nurse the babies. She may be frightened by the environment in which she is living. These situations can cause a sow to resorb a fetus so that no offspring are produced. When a sow has no babies, though these another. This makes it easier on any sow that may have had a large litter. To transfer the youngsters from one sow to the other the following methods usually prove successful. Wipe your hands over the foster mother and her offspring, then wipe the youngster(s) to be fostered. This will transfer some of the scent

If you do not have the time and resources required to properly raise a guinea pig family, then you should not breed your guinea pig.

were anticipated, this aspect should be considered; do not assume the sow is infertile.

## FOSTERING

If you have two or more guinea pigs with babies at the same time, and if there is a difference in the litter sizes, you can foster some of the youngsters from one sow to from the foster family onto the baby to be adopted. You could also rub some of the floor covering from the foster mother's hutch onto your hands and wipe these on the baby to be transferred.

## REARING

Rearing baby guinea pigs is not a problem as long as they are supplied with a well balanced diet. They are extremely fast moving little critters, so should you decide to let them exercise outdoors, they are best placed into a secure enclosure with a wire weld base. If left to run loose in your garden, that may be the last you will see of them! This of course applies even to adults, but to a lesser degree. As the youngsters approach four weeks of age they should be eating well on themselves and can be taken from their mother. Once this weaning process has been completed you can continue to offer them bread and milk for a while, because the calcium in the milk will still be needed if they are to develop good strong bones.

The more unique the color variety of your hamster the more likely you will have to pay more.

The youngsters can be placed into a large nursery pen with other babies, or you may prefer to keep them together as litters.

## ASSESSING YOUR STOCK

If you decide to breed guinea pigs, be sure that you will have the energy to maintain proper care. The best way to buy up stock is through pet shops, especially if you want a popular variety or color. Show quality examples can be sold via contacts made at exhibitions–a good breeder may even have a waiting list for certain individuals of a given standard, sex, or color.

Never let stock go if you have any doubts as to either its health, or the fact that it is not eating well. It is also very beneficial if you supply your customers with a basic care sheet, including items that it should be fed on. Obviously, you would assume they will purchase a book on guinea pigs, but not everyone does, so your care sheet may be the only source of reference they have on how they should look after their new pet. When selling stock try to discuss responsible ownership with people who visit you. Many of these may purchase inexpensive pets on the spur of the moment as gifts for children, but only to lose interest in them weeks later. Some would actually be better suited to keeping goldfish than guinea pigs, and such a fact may emerge if you talk to them about the time and care needed by guinea pigs.

You should not be overly concerned if the litter varies in markings and size.

The correct way to handle any guinea pig is to slide your palm under its body so that your fingers pass between its legs, thus giving it no leverage to spring from.

The more familiar you become with your guinea pig's behavior and habits, the easier it will be for you to determine when he is not feeling well.

# GENERAL CARE

Matters of general care, such as nutrition and health, have been dealt with in other chapters. Here we can look at such aspects as handling, grooming, transportation, and keeping guinea pigs with other pets.

## HANDLING

Guinea pigs are not in some ways the easiest of pets to handle. This has nothing to do with their nature, which is first class. They will rarely bite you even on occasions when this might be justified. A boar is perhaps not as forgiving of rough handling as is a sow, but even boars are very gentle if handled correctly. What must be remembered is that guinea pigs are very cautious creatures, so are easily startled. Following on from this is the fact that they may attempt to jump from your hands, and they are poorly built to land very well. With relatively large bodies, and short legs, they can easily injure their legs and head if they land from even a modest height.

When lifting a guinea pig up you should always support the weight of its chest and abdomen on the palm and wrist of your hand. Your free hand can then secure a gentle hold over its shoulders. In this way, the guinea pig's little legs will be dangling on either side of your hand, so are unable to gain leverage in order to jump. At the same time, feeling comfortable and secure, your pet will not be inclined to try to jump.

Children must be taught from the outset not to grasp at their pet with both hands, because it will certainly be able to wriggle and jump from them at the very moment they begin lifting it. As a result it will often be flipped onto its back when landing, for this is not an agile cat that can correct its fall in mid air. Once lifted, your pet can by all means be brought to your chest as a way of securing it.

## GROOMING

Smoothcoated varieties need virtually no grooming as their coat will stay in sparkling condition. Even so, you are recommended to groom them at least once a week as this helps them to get used to being handled. Always place your pet on a firm, non-slip surface when grooming it–on brown or white paper is a good idea. You can use a soft brush to gently remove any small bits of debris that may be clinging to the coat. If you are gentle they will enjoy this massage. Finish the job with a silk piece of cloth, or a chamois leather, which will leave the coat with a glossy sheen.

The longcoated varieties, such as Shelties and Peruvians, must be groomed every other day, at least, if their coat is to remain in a mat free state. Commence by giving the coat a brisk brushing which will remove debris and some of the tangles. Next, use a medium width comb and gently groom the fur. Should any tangles be felt do not pull at these, but tease them apart with your fingers, then brush them, and then comb again. By using this progressive method of grooming you will greatly reduce the risk of hurting the guinea pig, which will really make it dislike the whole process.

During the grooming of your pet, utilize the opportunity to check its ears and body for any signs of parasites. You can also check that its teeth are in good shape, and that its nails are not

**Not only do you have to maintain the cleanliness of your pet's hutch, but also the guinea pig! Bathing your guinea pig is simple and easy compared to cleaning other domestic pets.**

overgrown. Nails are normally not a problem in guinea pigs, but should they appear overlong they must be carefully trimmed. It is best to use the guillotine type clippers, which can be purchased at your pet store. Be very sure you do not trim too much of the nail otherwise it will bleed profusely, and this is very painful. If the claws are flesh colored you can easily see the blood vessel or "quick" and should trim

somewhat in front of this. If the claws are dark or black take even less off so you are working on the safe side.

**BATHING**

Normally, other than the longcoated varieties, a guinea pig will never need to be bathed. However, sometimes an individual may get itself in a mess, especially the lighter colored individuals and the roughcoated varieties, whose fur more readily gathers dirt. Bathing should always be done on warm days, and as early in the day as possible. This allows plenty of time for your pet to dry out before the evening.

Bathing can be done in a shallow bowl or in the kitchen sink. The water should be just warm, never too hot or too cold. Be very careful as you pour water over the fur that it does not get into your pet's eyes or ears, as this will certainly put off the whole procedure. Once the fur is saturated with water you can rub in a mild shampoo–one specially formulated for pets, but a baby shampoo will also be just fine.

The shampoo is then rinsed off with warm water. Be very sure this part of the bathing is done well. If not, the dried shampoo may irritate the skin of your pet. It also reduces the sheen, and can make the fur a little sticky. Gather up the guinea pig in a towel and give it a brisk rubbing down until it is dry. Your pet can then be placed in the garden on a sunny day, or it can be put in a large cardboard box, which has plenty of hay in it. This will keep

After a bath, be sure to thoroughly dry your guinea pig so it doesn't catch a cold.

it warm and will soon dry the fur. Putting it straight back in its hutch is not advised as the damp fur will merely become clogged with sawdust and any dirt in the hutch.

### TRANSPORTING GUINEA PIGS

Should you have a need to transport your guinea pig, for example in taking it to the vet, or to be cared for while you are on

you could scatter some oats on the floor. Always ensure that your pet has plenty of fresh air to breathe. Do not leave the carrying box in a car on a hot day as this can really stress your pet–and more than one has suffered death from heat stroke.

### LIVING WITH OTHER PETS

Guinea pigs, like rabbits, are among the most kindly animals

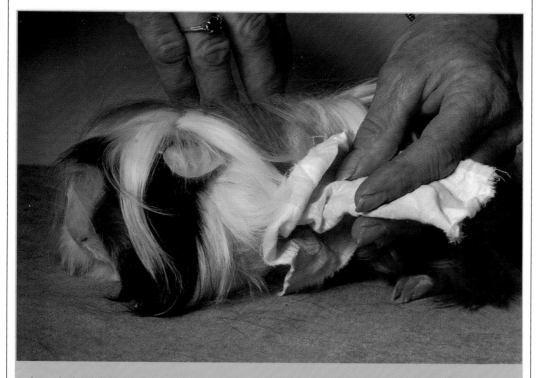

Longhaired guinea pigs that are shown must have their hair kept in wrappers to prevent it from getting soiled and matted.

vacation, the main criteria of a carry box is that it is secure and draftproof. You could use any of the inexpensive plastic transporters made for cats and small dogs, or one of the small fiberglass models. Line this with paper and hay. On a long journey

you could ever hope to own. They are never aggressive with other pets. This is especially so of guinea pigs who are almost defenseless when attacked. Their main means of defense is by scampering for cover at high speed–and they are very fast when they need to be. They will live quite happily alongside rabbits, which are the best companions they can have other than their own kind. If you have dogs or cats, you must be very watchful of these when your guinea pig is loose. Your pet is after all a rodent and as such, it falls within the natural prey of both dogs and cats.

Both of these predators have cats are familiar with your guinea pig they can become great friends and will get along very well. Even so, I would never leave dogs unattended with guinea pigs. I have known buck rabbits to turn and confront both dogs and cats, but guinea pigs do not do this. Always be on the alert when your pets are playing in your garden, where other animals might suddenly appear.

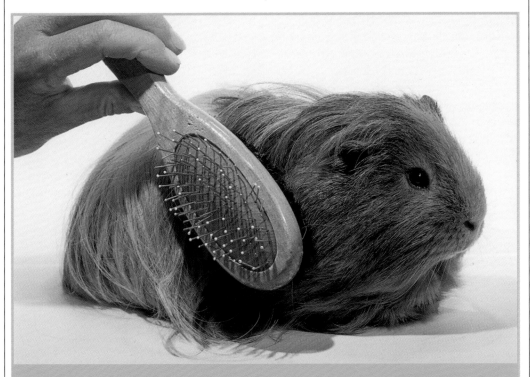

Grooming does more than improve the overall hygiene to your guinea pig, it also allows some time well spent with your pet.

very low hunting thresholds, which means it takes very little to prompt them to chase other animals. As a guinea pig tends to scurry around, this can excite dogs and cats and cause them to chase–even if only to play with– your cavy friend. Once dogs and

When in your home, take care that there is nothing low to the floor that might be injurious to your pet. A trailing wire to a table lamp, or an iron, for example, are potentially fatal if they fell on your guinea pig. Be sure external doors are closed, as your pet might wonder off or be hurt by the door should a gust of wind blow this shut. I have heard of rabbits being litter trained, but never a guinea pig, so do appreciate that when in your home your pet will leave a few droppings about. These are firm fecal pellets that are easily cleaned up, and are not smelly as are the feces of a dog or cat. Finally, do remember that guinea pigs always like to find a secure place to retreat to, so will likely get behind washing machines or refrigerators if they can. Such appliances are not easily moved to retrieve your pet, so block off access openings with a box or such. Should your guinea pig get itself into such a place it will often be case of waiting until it gets hungry and then placing a tasty morsel where it can sniff it. This usually brings it out!

## VACATIONS

If at all possible, arrange for a friend or neighbor to visit your home in order to feed your guinea pigs when you are on vacation. This is far better than boarding them in an establishment where they might contract an illness, regardless of how clean such a place may be. Your pets will always prefer to remain in their own home, where they feel secure. Ensure there is sufficient food left for them, and leave written instructions as to their feeding regimen. It is also wise to leave the phone number and address of your vet in a prominent place. Your guinea pig can be left for periods of up to 48 hours providing you ensure there are plenty of oats, bran, pellets and water available to it.

**Longhaired breeds can be easily groomed by children.**

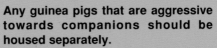

Any guinea pigs that are aggressive towards companions should be housed separately.

You should check every so often the teeth, nose, eyes, ears, and skin of the guinea pig.

# MAINTAINING HEALTH

Although it is perhaps a worn out cliche, the best way to maintain good health in your guinea pigs is to prevent illness from happening. While not all diseases and conditions can be prevented, even with sound husbandry, it is certainly true that most can. The vast majority of problems encountered by owners are attributable to neglect in one way or the other. To prevent illness it is therefore prudent to review the situations, or reasons, that create it in the first place. This gives us a good base from which to consider the best ways to avoid problems, if they can indeed be avoided.

## CAUSES OF DISEASE IN GUINEA PIGS

While a disease can suddenly strike your stock almost without warning, this situation is actually uncommon. More often the problem would not have occurred had there not been the conditions that enable pathogenic (disease causing) organisms to proliferate in large numbers to the point that they were able to overwhelm the natural defense mechanisms within all animals. The major causes of disease in any livestock are as follows.

1.) Lack of quarantine.
2.) Lack of hygiene.
3.) Feeding contaminated or unfresh food.
4.) Overcrowding.
5.) Stress.
6.) Poor accommodations.
7.) Delay in responding to visual signs of illness.
8.) Inherent genetic conditions.
9.) Injury.
10.) Incorrect acclimatization or convalescence.

A number of these causes are invariably linked together, in the same way that illness itself is often the result of more than one condition. There can be two or more pathogens working simultaneously.

One of the major problems in pet husbandry is that owners, having read about this or that disease and causal organism, will attempt a diagnosis and then treat it. They would be better off with no knowledge of these diseases, in which case they would be far more likely to seek the advice of their veterinarian whenever they felt something was wrong. During the passage of time the novice will invariably pick up knowledge of specific diseases, but initially he or she should concentrate all of their efforts into preventative husbandry.

## LACK OF QUARANTINE

This is one of the greatest causes of problems with those who own two or more guinea pigs or who own other pets like rabbits, and then add guinea pigs to their collection. When you purchase an extra animal, regardless of how good its former home, you cannot be sure whether or not it happens to be incubating some illness. If it is, this will quickly be contracted by any other stock it comes into contact with. If a guinea pig is a little out of condition, a move will certainly make matters worse. First, any move is traumatic to a greater or lesser degree. It will induce stress, and stress will draw nervous energy from the guinea pig. This will render it more susceptible to any bacteria that is new to it. It is unlikely that you will feed the guinea pig with quite the same foods as its former owner, and this may add to the stress situation.

Given these facts it makes sense to keep newly acquired stock isolated from other pets for a period of about 21 days. During this time, you can monitor its feeding habits and it will have time to make the adjustment from its former home without the added stress that might be caused by placing it with other stock. It will, at this time, encounter bacteria that is local to your area, indeed to your own home and stock. If these adversely affect it they should do so during the quarantine period.

## LACK OF HYGIENE

There is obviously a limit to the extent of time and cash any person can put into hygiene. After all, we cannot create a sterile environment for our stock as this would itself create increased health risks. However, certain basics should be observed. Cracked or chipped food containers should be discarded and replaced. All feeding utensils and dishes should be washed daily, and they should be numbered so they are always placed back into the same hutch.

Hutches should be thoroughly cleaned at least once every week, with care being taken to remove all soiled floor covering in the corners of the hutch. It must be disposed of–not left in the vicinity of the hutches. When handling ill stock it is wise to invest in disposable surgical gloves. If not, then always wash your hands before handling any other guinea pigs or other pets. With this in mind it is certainly beneficial if water is supplied to the building that accommodates your stock.

## FEEDING UNFRESH FOODS

While the life of dry foods, such as oats and pellets, is relatively long, this only applies if they are kept in a dry state. Even so, it is not wise to store foods for any length of time. Do not buy in bulk such that this means keeping the foods for months at a time. Greenfoods readily deteriorate, as do supplements such as vitamins. If at all unsure about a given food it should be discarded. Choose your food supplier with care, because it is obviously important that they are storing bulk foods correctly.

## OVERCROWDING

Exactly what constitutes overcrowding is difficult to be precise about, because to a large degree it depends on what state of hygiene is being observed, and what facility there is in the building (ventilation, ionizers etc). Overcrowding is not simply a

To prevent serious diseases from spreading, it is important that you know what effect they will have on your cavy and what it will look like when it is ill.

Many health matters can be avoided simply by being aware of your pet on an individual basis.

case of how many guinea pigs are in a single hutch, but also how many there are in a given building. They do not have to be in the same hutch for a disease to sweep through the entire stock if they are all sharing the same building.

Obviously, the more guinea pigs that are placed in a single hutch, the greater the risk of direct contact transmission of pathogens. If the guinea pigs are short of space to move about in, they are more likely to squabble and suffer injury from fighting. This induces stress, thus raises the risk of illness.

### STRESS

This is a condition that is very difficult to recognize, thus treat. Its effect on the individual is to use up nervous energy and to interrupt normal metabolic processes, such as nutrition and the ability to relax. This reduces the animal's natural defense mechanisms against illness. Stress may be caused by a multitude of situations. For example, noise, close proximity to an aggressive companion, a diet that fails to meet the psychological needs of the animal, or being placed in unfamiliar surroundings. It is closely linked to fear, but is a quite distinct condition. Fear results from a direct threat that is momentarily present, stress is an ongoing situation that may not result from any obvious threat. All that you can do to prevent this is to remove any conditions that you think might cause it, such as those mentioned.

### POOR ACCOMMODATIONS

This is obviously linked to other items discussed, but also includes any housing that is damp, is subjected to excess direct sunlight, to extremes in temperature, or that gives access to vermin. Any of these will increase the risk of illness.

### DELAY IN RESPONSE TO VISUAL SIGNS OF ILLNESS

This is often a prelude to increased severity of an illness, and encompasses two distinct aspects. To recognize an illness entails not only seeing obvious clinical signs, but also appreciating any change in behavior. The behavior is usually, though not always, the first sign that something is wrong. In order to appreciate a change you must be aware of what is normal for each individual guinea pig you own. To do this you must spend an amount of time studying your stock–and a busy hobbyist with a large stock may not always have the time needed.

You should always observe your stock when it eats. By so doing you will know which are the greedy eaters, and those which are best described as delicate or "picky" feeders. You will know which are the outgoing type of guinea pigs, and those which are rather shy. Any change from their behavior would obviously suggest something is causing this change.

In terms of clinical signs the

following are all indicative of a problem:

Weeping eyes and runny nose.

Noisy breathing–any wheezing sounds.

Excessive scratching.

Sickness.

Liquid fecal matter, especially if it is streaked with blood.

Any sore or bald spots on the body.

Loss of fur.

Convulsions.

Abrasions and lumps on the body.

Loss of sheen to the coat.

If more than one of these signs is observed it will usually indicate a more serious condition. The answer, once a sign is seen, is to isolate the guinea pig immediately–not to wait a day or so to see if things improve. This merely increases the risk that the problem will spread to other stock. Once the animal is isolated you can then observe it more carefully. You can give it a thorough physical check to start with, and then place it in a warm environment. Heat will usually correct any minor chill, so an infrared lamp set up in front of a hospital cage can often work wonders. Place it towards one end so the guinea pig can move away from the hottest point if it so desires–you do not want to induce stress. Next you should telephone your vet and discuss the matter with him or her.

## INHERENT GENETIC CONDITIONS

The genes of your guinea pig can adversely affect its health in one of three ways. They may be linked to a deformity, or to a congenital condition that cannot be cured. In a more general way they will control the general vigor of the individual. A highly inbred animal may be much more susceptible to given illnesses than one which is less inbred. However, inbred animals may also be more vigorous than the average of the population, so do not make the error that many make of assuming inbreeding automatically reduces the vigor of an animal. That it may do so in most instances is because the original stock was faulty to start with, and inbreeding merely highlights the fault that was already there.

## INJURY

This can range from a minor cut, to broken limbs, burns and any other physical injury. Once any animal is injured its resistance to disease is obviously lowered, so it is essential that the injury is treated promptly by your vet. Many diseases can be caused by secondary infection setting in to what might only be, initially, a minor lesion. Never leave skin abrasions untreated. They should be carefully washed, then treated with a suitable antiseptic powder, ointment or liquid.

If left exposed, they are prime sites for bacterial colonization and access to the bloodstream. This transposes the condition from external to internal, and will invariably result in a much more serious situation. The main cause of skin abrasions will be scratching or minor cuts.

Scratches are usually the result of either an insect bite, or of external parasites such as lice, mites and fleas. Regular inspection of the skin should be done to check for parasites. All of these are easily eradicated with modern treatments.

Fleas and mites will breed off the host in its accommodations. Lice spend their whole life cycle on the host. These parasites can arrive on your stock from various sources, such as other pets, on your clothes, by wind dispersal, and so on. They will only reach a state of infestation if you are lax on hygiene, and in failing to inspect your stock on a regular basis.

Baths are essential to remove dirt and lice from its coat.

### INCORRECT ACCLIMATIZATION OR CONVALESCENCE

When you acquire a guinea pig do bear in mind that when it changes homes, it is probable that there will be some degree of change in the temperatures it is familiar with. If it came from a pet store, or from a breeder, whose housing was maintained at a higher temperature than its new accommodations, there would be every chance of it contracting a chill if you did not acclimatize it correctly. Equally well, if it was from stock kept outdoors, and you placed it into a hot indoor accommodation this might cause it to react in some way. Any potential temperature differences should thus be considered and catered for. Acclimatization periods can range from a few days to a few weeks, depending on the type of accommodation and the time of the year, thus the temperature differencial.

Should a guinea pig become ill it is as important to ensure it is fully recovered as it was to isolate it in the first place. All too often an owner, assuming their pet has recovered, places it back into its quarters too soon. The first thing to be sure of is that the treatment given by your vet has been completed. Do not discontinue with this just because your pet appears to have fully recovered, this could be a mistake. Should any bacteria have survived the shortened treatment, they may develop immunity to the medicines, which would mean a relapse and more difficulty in treating them a second time.

## HELPING YOUR VET

Should one of your guinea pigs become ill it will be a great help to your vet if you are able to furnish certain information. This will help in the diagnosis. Among the data you should have at hand when you talk to the vet is the following:

When was the condition first noticed?

Are any others of your stock or pets displaying similar symptoms?

How long have you owned the guinea pig, and how old is it?

Have any of your stock been ill recently?

Is the guinea pig feeding normally?

What is the state of its fecal matter? Normal or loose?

Is it moving about normally?

How many other pets or guinea pigs do you have?

Are there any piles of rotting vegetation near the hutch?

Have you changed food supplier recently–for oats and such?

Is there any chance the guinea pig may have ingested poison or some foreign matter?

Have you acquired any other stock recently?

Have you visited any locations from which the illness could have been transported by you (on your clothes)? Such places would include exhibitions, pet shops, other breeders, even a vet's surgery.

Any of these aspects may have some bearing on the problem, thus the treatment given.

## TREATMENTS

The potential range of treatments for illnesses in your guinea pigs is considerable these days. For minor abrasions there are many antiseptic powders and lotions available, while styptic pencils and potassium permanganate crystals will both stem minor blood loss from cuts. Your veterinarian has a range of antibiotics that can be used for both specific and non-specific problems. Surgery is also possible. Fungal disease (ringworm) is one of the more difficult conditions to treat as it is protracted, and the spores are able to live considerable periods in the accommodations.

There are numerous worms that can infest the digestive system of guinea pigs, but all can be treated with modern drugs. In order to greatly reduce the incidence of disease or unhealthy conditions, it is certainly worthwhile taking your guinea pig to the vet for periodic inspection. The vet may notice something you did not. If you have a stud of guinea pigs it is advised that the vet visits you periodically to look over your stock. He or she may be able to suggest improvements in management based on observations of your layout and method of storage of food.

# GUINEA PIG VARIETIES

If you are interested in becoming a breeder of guinea pigs, or if you just want to see all the colors and variations seen in these delightful pets before you choose one, you should visit a major exhibition. The range is vast and far more extensive than might be thought purely by seeing what is available in your local pet shop.

Guinea pigs are divided into two broad categories, these being the selfs and the non-selfs. A self animal of any species is one which has a single color, such as black, red, or chocolate. It will breed true to its color when paired to its own kind. However, in guinea pigs, somewhat more is implied in the term self. It also indicates the coat type. The self is a smoothcoated variety.

The non-selfs may be self colored, and they may be smoothcoated, but not both. For example, the beautiful Roans and Dalmatians, as well as the Tortoiseshell and White, are smoothcoated, but of course they are two or three colored. The Abyssinian may be a self red, but its coat is rough rather than smooth. Likewise, the Peruvian may be self colored, but its coat is very long. Apart from the rough and longcoated varieties there are also Rex and Satin guinea pigs, as well as those which sport crests on their heads. When these

An American Crested (left) and Golden White guinea pig outdoors.

various coat mutations are combined with the available colors, the potential range to choose from is enormous. If you plan to breed with your guinea pigs, it is advised that you try and specialize in just one or two varieties. It is far better to excel in what you do than to try and breed many color varieties, and have to settle for a lesser standard. Most colors are readily available, but you may have to search to locate certain colors and coat types that are relatively new, such as Satin or Rex.

Although some of the colors are not yet seen in all coat types, do bear in mind that they are possible. Coat type and color are not genetically linked. Likewise, any guinea pig can be bred with a crest.

## SELF VARIETIES

There about twelve colors to be seen in the self guinea pigs, and the list is growing. The standard in terms of type is extremely high in this group, it being the oldest of the guinea pig varieties. The coat is relatively short and very glossy. That of the sow is somewhat softer than that of the boar, so sows are especially popular with exhibitors.

## NEW SELF COLORS

There are always new colors being developed, and among these are the saffron, which is within the cream range. The blue

A White (left) and Golden White guinea pig running loose on a deck.

A Blue Point (left) and Tri-Color guinea pig at play.

is gaining popularity. You may find it difficult to distinguish between some of the new colors because they are, of necessity, actually variations of reds, or chocolate, for example. As breeders are able to establish greater control of the modifying genes, they are able to standardize on a color shade, thus it becomes an accepted color variety.

## NON-SELF VARIETIES

It is within the non-selfs that the guinea pigs with two or more colors are found. This group also contains those with non-smooth coats. It is thus in the non-selfs that most new varieties, as they are recognized, will tend to be found.

## NON-SELF COLORS

The remainder of the non-selfs varieties comprise all smoothcoated guinea pigs in which two or more colors are present. A number of these are long established, while others are still in the rare category, and are not officially recognized as varieties, so are exhibited as Any Other Variety (AOV).

## BI AND TRICOLORS

While the Tortie and Tortie and white are well established varieties, it is also possible to produce similar marked guinea pigs of other colors. A black and white combination would be a bicolor, as would a chocolate and lemon. The addition of white would of course create the tricolor.

## OTHER VARIETIES

Among the latest of guinea pig varieties is the Satin, in which the coat has an extremely high satin-like gloss. Another coat variation is the Ridgeback which, as the name would suggest, sports a ridge of harsh hair along its back.

## WHAT OF THE FUTURE?

In the coming years you can expect to see other coat types appearing, though some of these might be of the grotesque type that parallel the Sphinx, or hairless cat. A long eared guinea pig is another possibility, but it is hoped that breeders will not support varieties that, due to the abnormality of the mutation, make life for the guinea pig more arduous. Unfortunately, if the past record in pets generally is reviewed, some breeders show little concern for the well being of their pets when new mutations are discovered–let's hope you do not fall within this category. In terms of coat patterns it would seem quite possible that a striped guinea pig may one day be produced, as might a genuine blue if a dilution gene were to appear. Presently, the so-called blues are really black guinea pigs with silver, as in the blue Roan and the slate blue. We may yet see medium length coated guinea pigs sporting colors that equate the beautiful smokes and cameos seen in cats, or those with the

The eyes are partly shut on this smooth Tortoiseshell and White guinea pig.

plush velvet-like rex coats seen in rabbits. The future is thus full of potential for these unassuming little rodents.

## CREATING NEW VARIETIES

A new variety of guinea pig is created in one of two ways. Either a new mutation appears that alters the coat, a body part, or the color of the guinea pig, or existing breeds and colors are crossed in order to transpose one or more mutations from one variety to another. Sometimes the effect is pleasing, at other times it is not, or merely creates problems. Color breeding in particular is a fascinating and very popular part of the hobby. However, in any form of experimental breeding it should be appreciated that more often than, not the failure rate is far more likely than the success.

When crossing varieties to produce new ones, the result will be a large number of offspring that are mongrels having only pet value. Experimental breeding can thus be a very costly undertaking, the more so because such a large number of

Guinea pigs, like these two, will provide all owners many years of companionship.

offspring must be retained until they are old enough to make decisions on their future breeding worth. If you are interested in this form of breeding you are recommended to join the rare breeds club of your country in order to see what the potential is in the newer varieties. Should you be fortunate enough to find a new mutation among your offspring, do contact your national guinea pig club and tell them about it. They will be in a position to place you in contact with a geneticist who can advise you what is the best course of action to take in respect of future matings.

In all forms of experimental breeding it is crucial that you maintain very detailed records, as these will be essential for reference purposes as you establish the mutation or hybrid.

**A Lilac sow.**

An American Crested guinea pig nibbling on some green apples.